# EASY SPEAKING
## ENGLISH FOR CHILDREN

### Written by Concita Brito-D'Orta

**Easy Speaking Volume 1**
**Copyright © 2021 by Concita Brito-D'Orta**
**Reviewed by the author**

Book and Cover illustration designed by Freepik
**Book Designer:**
Jader Junior

Easy Speaking Volume 1 is a work of fiction. Any resemblance to actual events, places, incidents, or persons, living or dead is entirely coincidental.

All rights reserved.

No part of this book may be used or reproduced in any manner whatsoever without the express written permission of the author.

**ISBN: 978-0-578-84311-7**
**Printed in the United States of America**
www.easyspeaking.net

## ACKNOWLEDGEMENT

All praise and glory to my Lord Almighty for his richest grace and mercy for the accomplishment of this book. I am extremely thankful to my parents for their love, prayers, caring and sacrifices for educating me for my future. I am very much thankful to my daughter Nahla, and my son Issa for their love, understanding and continuing support to complete this work.
I wish to express my deep gratitude to my awesome husband, Augustine. From reading early drafts to proofreading and giving me advice on the little details of my book. He was an important part of this project.
Thank You All!

# INDEX

| | |
|---|---|
| Lesson 1 | 7 |
| Lesson 2 | 8 |
| Lesson 3 | 10 |
| Lesson 4 | 11 |
| Lesson 5 | 12 |
| Lesson 6 | 13 |
| Lesson 7 | 14 |
| Lesson 8 | 15 |
| Lesson 9 | 16 |
| Lesson 10 | 18 |
| Lesson 11 | 20 |
| Lesson 12 | 23 |
| Lesson 13 | 25 |
| Lesson 14 | 26 |
| Lesson 15 | 29 |
| Lesson 16 | 30 |
| Lesson 17 | 31 |
| Lesson 18 | 32 |
| Lesson 19 | 33 |
| Lesson 20 | 35 |
| Lesson 21 | 36 |
| Lesson 22 | 38 |
| Lesson 23 | 40 |
| Lesson 24 | 42 |
| Lesson 25 | 44 |
| Lesson 26 | 46 |
| Lesson 27 | 48 |
| Lesson 28 | 49 |
| Lesson 29 | 50 |
| Lesson 30 | 51 |
| Lesson 31 | 52 |
| Lesson 32 | 53 |
| Lesson 33 | 54 |
| Lesson 34 | 55 |
| Lesson 35 | 56 |
| Lesson 36 | 57 |
| Lesson 37 | 58 |

# CLASSROOM LANGUAGE

**YES**  **NO**  **STOP**  **RAISE YOUR HAND**

**LINE UP**

**BE QUIET**  **SIT**  **EAT**

## MOUTH POSITION ALPHABET
### Use these pictures to help you pronounce the letter sounds.

A, E, I

Ch, J, Sh

L

F, V

B, M, P

U

Th

R
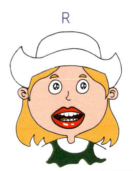

O

W, Q

C, D, G, H, K, N, S, T, X, Y, Z

## I CAN READ: Look at the picture point to the letters and follow the mouth alphabet.

C     A     T

P     I     G

B     E     D

C     A     B

H     A     T

D     O     G

                        M          O          P

                        R          A          T

                        H          A          M

                        M          A          T

                        B          A          T

# WHAT IS THE WORD? Look at the picture, follow the mouth alphabet and write the word.

_____  _____  _____

_____  _____  _____

_____  _____  _____

_____  _____  _____

_____  _____  _____

## ANSWER THE QUESTIONS USING: IT IS A ...

1. What is it?

_____

2. What is it?

_____

3. What is it?

_____

4. What is it?

_____

5. What is it?

_____

6. What is it?

_____

7. What is it?

_____

8. What is it?

_____

9. What is it?

_____

## BOY OR GIRL? Look at the picture and choose BOY or GIRL

 BOY

 GIRL

Ⓐ BOY   Ⓑ GIRL

Ⓐ BOY   Ⓑ GIRL

Ⓐ BOY   Ⓑ GIRL

Ⓐ BOY   Ⓑ GIRL

Ⓐ BOY   Ⓑ GIRL

Ⓐ BOY   Ⓑ GIRL

## HE OR SHE?
## Look at the picture and write HE or SHE

HE　　　　　　　　　　　SHE

# Lesson 7

## HE OR SHE?
Look at the picture and write in COMPLETE SENTENCES. Follow the example: HE IS BOB. HE IS A DOCTOR.

**1. Lisa/ teacher**

**2. Diana/ dentist**

**3. John/ lawyer**

**4. Peter/ singer**

## ABOUT ME
## Choose and write

**I AM A ...**

____ Girl                    ____ Boy

I am a ...

_____

My name is ...

_____

# FEELINGS – HOW ARE YOU TODAY?

Happy                Angry                Sad

Scared               Confused             Surprised

I am ...

_____

# Lesson 9

## LOOK AT THE PICTURE AND ANSWER THE QUESTIONS IN COMPLETE SENTENCES

**1. Are you confused OR sad?**

_____

**2. Are you scared OR surprised?**

_____

**3. Are you happy OR angry?**

_____

**4. Are you angry OR sad?**

_____

**5. Are you happy OR confused?**

_____

**6. Are you surprised OR scared?**

_____

Lesson 10

## PARTS OF MY BODY

**1. Write the correct word under the picture.**

          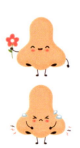

_____                  _____

_____    _____

_____

**Draw a picture of yourself.**

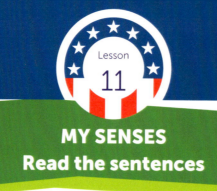

## MY SENSES
### Read the sentences

## My Five Senses

 I can see with my eyes

 I can hear with my ears

 I can smell with my nose

 I can taste with my tongue

 I can touch with my hands

# MATCH EACH PICTURE WITH THE CORRECT SENSE

## Match the Pictures

**USE THE WORDS BELOW TO COMPLETE THE SENTENCES:**
EYE - SKIN - EAR - NOSE - TONGUE - TASTE - FEEL - SEE - HEAR - SMELL

1. I use my _____ to _____

2. I use my _____ to _____

3. I use my _____ to _____

4. I use my _____ to _____

5. I use my _____ to _____

## BACK TO SCHOOL
### Write the word under the picture

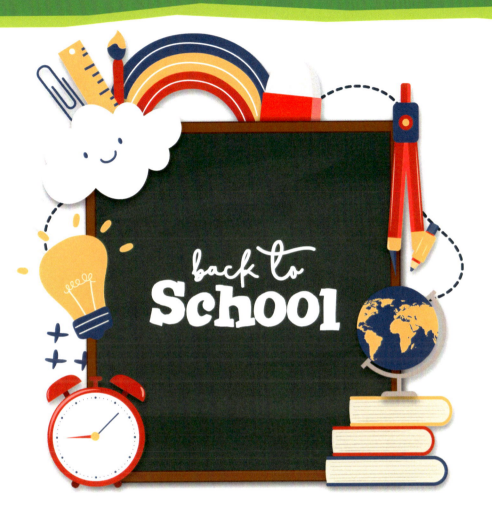

Pencil

Notebook

## Lesson 12

Pencil case

School bag

Ruler

Sharpener

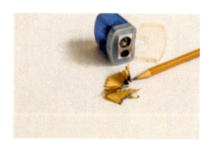

Pen

Glue

**Lesson 13**

## YES OR NO? — Answer the questions. Use the words from the word bank: YES, IT IS/ NO, IT IS NOT/ Or IT IS A …

**Is it a pen or a pencil sharpener?**

_____

**Is it a pencil?**

_____

**What is it?**

_____

**Is it a ruler?**

_____

**Is it a pencil case or a backpack?**

_____

**What is it?**

_____

# I SEE MY COLORS
## Read the sentence and choose your answer

Red  Green  Yellow
Brown  Blue  Black
Pink  Purple

**It is a blue umbrella.**

Ⓐ  Ⓑ

## It is a green car.

Ⓐ　　　　　　　　　　　Ⓑ

## It is a red boot

Ⓐ　　　　　　　　　　　Ⓑ

## It is a purple hat.

Ⓐ　　　　　　　　　　　Ⓑ

**It is a brown dog.**

Ⓑ

**It is a pink balloon.**

Ⓑ

## WHAT COLOR?
Look at the picture and answer the question using IT IS ...

1. What color is the apple?

_____

2. What color is the sun?

_____

3. What color is the pencil?

_____

4. What color is the car?

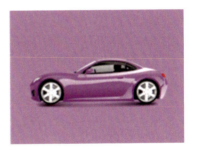

_____

5. What color is the lunch box?

_____

Lesson 16

## HOW MANY?
Count each set of objects below and write the correct number under the pictures

# Lesson 17

## ANSWER THE QUESTIONS

Follow the example: **WHAT DO YOU SEE?**

I see five books.

_____  _____

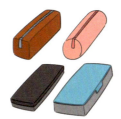  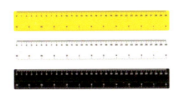  

_____  _____  _____

# WHAT DO YOU SEE?

I see one red strawberry.

**Look at the picture and answer the question: WHAT DO YOU SEE?**

1 _____
2 _____
3 _____
4 _____
5 _____
6 _____
7 _____
8 _____
9 _____

## Lesson 19

## WHAT IS IT?
### Choose your answer

**1. What is it?**

Ⓐ It is a fish.

Ⓑ It is a fox.

**2. What is it?**

Ⓐ It is a tiger.

Ⓑ It is a goat.

**3. What is it?**

Ⓐ It is a duck.

Ⓑ It is a frog.

**Lesson 19**

**4. What is it?**

Ⓐ It is a bunny.

Ⓑ It is a fish.

**5. What is it?**

Ⓐ It is a goat.

Ⓑ It is a cow.

**6. What is it?**

Ⓐ It is a tiger.

Ⓑ It is a horse.

**7. What is it?**

Ⓐ It is a hen.

Ⓑ It is a cat.

# Lesson 20

## WHO OR WHAT?

WHO is for PEOPLE

WHAT is for THINGS

**Write WHO IS SHE/HE? Or WHAT IS IT?**

1. She is Jen. _____
2. It is a book. _____
3. It is a dog. _____
4. He is Robert. _____
5. It is a school bag. _____
6. She is Lisa. _____
7. It is a pencil. _____
8. He is Sam. _____

Lesson 21

## DO YOU LIKE …? Answer the questions using YES, I DO or NO, I DON'T.

1. Do you like pizza?

_____

2. Do you like ice cream?

_____

3. Do you like broccoli?

_____

4. Do you like popcorn?

_____

5. Do you like French fries?

_____

6. Do you like donuts?

_____

### Lesson 21

**7. Do you like cereal?**

_____

**8. Do you like pancakes?**

_____

**9. Do you like spaghetti?**

_____

**10. Do you like salad?**

_____

**11. Do you like yogurt?**

_____

**12. Do you like orange juice?**

_____

# Lesson 22

## WHO WEARS …?
## Answer the questions using: HE DOES OR SHE DOES.

This is Anna. She is a girl. This is Bill. He is a boy.

1. Who wears a dress? He does or She does?

_____

2. Who wears a bow tie?

_____

3. Who wears a skirt?

_____

4. Who wears a shirt?

_____

5. Who wears a swimsuit?

_____

6. Who wears a suit?

_____

7. Who wears a blouse?

_____

## CLOTHING

## CLOTHING

MATCH EACH PICTURE WITH THE CORRECT WORD.

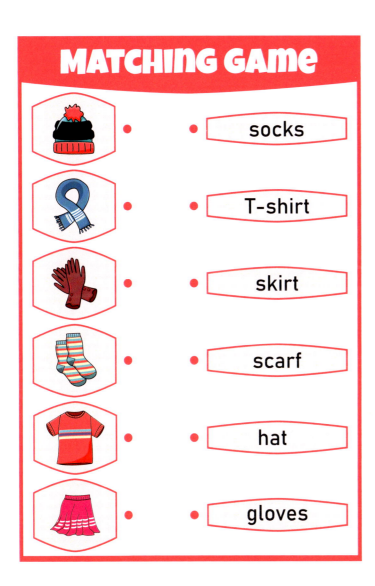

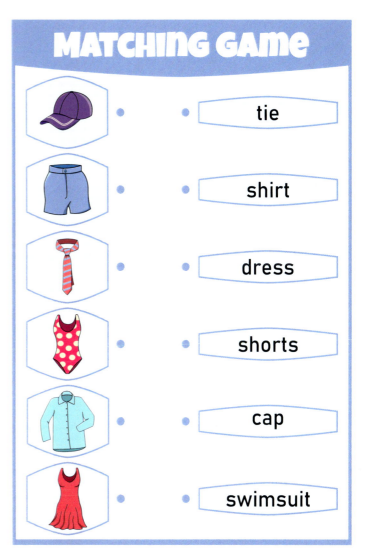

# SEASONS

SPRING

SUMMER

AUTUMN

WINTER

In summer — we go to the beach.

In fall — the leaves fall from the trees.

In winter — it snows.

In spring  the flowers grow.

**ANSWER THE QUESTIONS:**

1. What is your favorite season?

   _____

2. Do you wear flip flops OR jeans in fall?

   _____

3. What do you wear in winter?

   _____

4. Do you wear bikinis OR gloves in summer?

   _____

5. What do you wear in spring?

   _____

Lesson 25

## WHERE? Where is for places.

**Choose your answer:**

**1. Where are you going?**

Ⓐ I am going to the bank.
Ⓑ She is going to the supermarket

**2. Where is he going?**

Ⓐ I am going to school.
Ⓑ He is going to school.

## Lesson 25

**3. Where are you going?**

Ⓐ I am going to the zoo.
Ⓑ She is going to school.

**4. Where is he going?**

Ⓐ I am going to the pool.
Ⓑ He is going to the pool.

**5. Where is he going?**

Ⓐ He is going to the shopping mall.
Ⓑ She is going to the pool.

**6. Where are you going?**

Ⓐ She is going to the zoo.
Ⓑ I am going to the park.

Lesson 26

## ANSWER THE QUESTIONS IN COMPLETE SENTENCES

### Use words from the word bank:

| Yes, it is. | Yes, she is. | Yes, he is. | Yes, I do. |
| No, it is not. | No, she is not. | No, he is not. | No, I don't. |
| It is a ... | She is a ... | He is a ... | Yes, I am. |
|  |  |  | No, I am not. |
|  |  |  | I am a ... |

1. Is it a frog or a dog?

2. Are you a boy or a girl?

3. Is it a fish?

_____

_____

_____

4. What is it?

5. Is it a bed?

6. Do you like salad?

_____

_____

_____

7. Is it a pool or a park?

8. Is David a boy or a girl?

9. Is Laura a girl?

10. Are you at the zoo?

11. Is it a pancake?

## I CAN READ AND ANSWER QUESTIONS ABOUT THE STORY

# The Cat

I see a cat.
The cat likes to play with a ball of yarn.
The cat is brown and white.
The cat is big.

**1. I see a …**

Ⓐ goat  Ⓑ cat

**2. The cat likes to …**

Ⓐ play with a ball of yarn.  Ⓑ jump.

**3. What color is the cat?**

_____

**4. The cat is …**

Ⓐ little  Ⓑ big

## READ AND ANSWER THE QUESTIONS

I see a pumpkin.
The pumpkin is big and orange.
I like orange pumpkins.

**1. The story is about:**

Ⓐ cake     Ⓑ pumpkin     Ⓒ apple

**2. I see …**

Ⓐ a pumpkin     Ⓑ an apple     Ⓒ a banana

**3. The pumpkin is …**

Ⓐ little and red     Ⓑ big and blue     Ⓒ big and orange

## READ AND ANSWER THE QUESTIONS

Bingo is a monkey.
Bingo can read a book.
Bingo likes to eat bananas.

**1. What is Bingo?**

Ⓐ a monkey    Ⓑ a cat    Ⓒ a bunny

**2. What can Bingo do?**

Ⓐ swim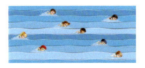

Ⓑ sing     Ⓒ read

**3. What does Bingo like to eat?**

Ⓐ fish    Ⓑ bananas    Ⓒ apples

## READ AND ANSWER THE QUESTIONS

Gina is my friend.
She has a teddy bear.
Her dad gave it to her.
She loves her teddy bear.

**1. Gina is …**

Ⓐ my teacher   Ⓑ my friend   Ⓒ my sister

**2. She has …**

Ⓐ teddy bears   Ⓑ dolls   Ⓒ a teddy bear

**3. Her _____ gave it to her.**

Ⓐ aunt   Ⓑ mom   Ⓒ dad

## READ AND ANSWER THE QUESTIONS

**THE ZOO**

I see Mary and Jane.
They are going to the zoo.
They are going to see the giraffes.
They love the giraffes.

**Write your answers:**

1. What do you see?

_____

2. Where are they going?

_____

3. What are they going to see?

_____

## READ AND ANSWER THE QUESTIONS

**SOCCER**

I have a friend.
His name is Tim.
He likes to play soccer.
He plays soccer every Sunday.

**1. I have a friend and his name is** _____
Ⓐ Greg   Ⓑ John   Ⓒ Tim

**2. He likes to** _____
Ⓐ play piano   Ⓑ play soccer   Ⓒ ride a bike

**3. He plays every** _____
Ⓐ Monday   Ⓑ Saturday   Ⓒ Sunday

## READ AND ANSWER THE QUESTIONS

**THE FROG**

Linda can see a little frog.
The frog can hop.
It can swim too.
Linda is happy to see a little frog.

**COMPLETE THE SENTENCES. WRITE YOUR ANSWERS.**

1. The frog can hop and _____

2. Linda likes the _____

3. Linda is _____ to see a little frog.

## READ AND ANSWER THE QUESTIONS

**HAPPY LION**

I see a lion.
His name is Leo.
Leo is big and brown.
Leo is very happy.

1. What do you see?

  Ⓐ          Ⓑ          Ⓒ

2. What is the lion's name?

_____

3. Leo is _____ and _____

Lesson 35

## READ AND ANSWER THE QUESTIONS

This is a snowman.
His name is Frosty.
He loves the snow.
His nose is orange.

**1. What is the snowman's name?**

_____

**2. What does Frosty love?**

_____

**3. What color is Frosty's nose?**

_____

## READ AND ANSWER THE QUESTIONS

I love cupcakes.
I am eating a vanilla cupcake.
My mom baked them for me.
The cupcakes are sweet and soft.

**1. What am I eating?**

_____

**2. The cupcakes are _____ and _____**

_____

_____

**3. Who baked the cupcakes for me?**

Ⓐ my dad    Ⓑ my mom    Ⓒ my sister

## OPINION WRITING

**CUPCAKE**    **OR**    **BIRTHDAY CAKE**

**DO YOU LIKE CUPCAKES OR BIRTHDAY CAKE?**

_____

because _____

_____

_____

## This Award Is Presented To

_____

**for**

 **Doing Your Best**

 **Trying Hard**

 **Not Giving Up**

 **Making a Great Effort**